Mei Fuh

Memories from China

Dedicated to Mei Yong, Mei Oe,
and all who share my early memories of China
—E.S.

Text copyright © 1998 by Edith Schaeffer
Illustrations copyright © 1998 by Lesley Liu

The text of this book is set in Galliard.
The illustrations are pen and ink on paper.

Library of Congress Cataloging-in-Publication Data

Schaeffer, Edith.
Mei fuh: memories from China / by Edith Schaeffer; illustrated by Lesley Liu.
p. cm.
Summary: Recounts the lives of an American girl and her family living in China
in the early 1900s, with details about food, home life, servants, and customs.
ISBN 0-395-72290-X
[1. China—Fiction. 2. Family life—China—Fiction.] I. Liu, Lesley, ill. II. Title.
PZ7.S52726Bab 1998
[Fic]—DC21 97-10126 CIP AC

Manufactured in the United States of America
RRD 10 9 8 7 6 5 4 3 2 1

Mei Fuh
Memories from China

Edith Schaeffer

Illustrations by **Lesley Liu**

Houghton Mifflin Company
Boston 1998

Two Birthdays

A very long time ago, a baby girl was born in China, and her parents named her Mei Fuh. In the Chinese language, Mei Fuh means "beautiful happiness." The tiny new baby was washed carefully, dressed, and then put into her mother's arms. She slept peacefully as her mother cuddled her. Mei Fuh's father patted her gently and kissed her mother. Then he ran down the staircase and hurried away to get into a rickshaw that took him down the cobblestone street.

Mei Fuh was born on November 3, 1914. Because her parents were American, her birth had to be registered in Washington, D.C. This was before telephones could reach people across the ocean, so Mei Fuh's father sent a cablegram to Washington, and all the important facts about her birth were written down in a record book there. The time difference meant that the message arrived in Washington on November 2, 1914, and that is what the man wrote down as Mei Fuh's birthday. So Mei Fuh became an American citizen, and her American name was Edith Rachel. But everyone in China called her Mei Fuh—even her mother and father—and she always had her birthday parties on November 3.

Mei Fuh and her family lived in the city of Wenchow on the coast of southern China. They lived in a compound, which is a piece of land surrounded by high walls. The walls kept the people inside safe, because China could be a dangerous place in those days.

The compound was like a small village. Inside its walls were bamboo trees, grass, flowers, and a swing for Mei Fuh. There was a boarding school for Chinese boys and another one for Chinese girls. Mei Fuh's parents taught in those schools. Mei Fuh lived in a big house with two stairways with fine mahogany banisters. On one side, the stairway led to the bedrooms of Mei Fuh's family: mother, father, and two sisters. The other stairway led to rooms belonging to women who were teachers at the school. There were little houses, too, for teachers and for other people who worked in the compound, like Adjipah, the gatekeeper, and Wong, the cook. There was also a church with a Chinese pastor, and he had his own little house.

When Mei Fuh learned to sit up and then to crawl she was put into a kind of Chinese playpen called a *gatse*. The gatse had a round floor and sides made of bamboo poles. The poles were placed close together so that she could not put her head through and they were smooth so that her small hands could slide up and down them. Holding on to the poles, Mei Fuh learned to stand up and to walk round and round in a little circle. Sometimes she went up and down on her toes, almost like a dance. All her life, Mei Fuh loved the feel of bamboo.

Baby Mei Fuh had a bamboo rattle, a fat little

bamboo whistle, and a cloth doll that her mother had made her. She also had a soft ball made by a girl who lived in the compound. The schoolgirls made beautiful linen tablecloths and embroidered baby clothes. Out of the leftover scraps they made wonderful balls by winding thin strips of fabric and string round and round. The outside layer was all different colors of silk, linen, cotton, and string woven in a lovely pattern.

Mei Fuh's parents were busy teaching, so she had a Chinese nanny, an Amah, to take care of her. In fact, almost everyone Mei Fuh knew was Chinese, so she could speak Chinese before she could speak English.

This was Mei Fuh's world—a compound where everyone was her friend.

Outside the Compound

In one wall of the compound was the big front gate with a heavy handle to open it and a heavy lock to keep it shut. Adjipah unlocked the gate to let people in and out. The gate had a window with crisscross bars. Sometimes Adjipah lifted Mei Fuh so she could look out and see what was going on in the street and on the canal that ran next to the street.

Mei Fuh saw people carrying baskets of fish or cabbages or live chickens on their heads. They balanced the baskets by standing and walking very straight and holding their heads in just the right way. She saw little babies being carried on their mothers' backs. She saw all sorts of people riding in rickshaws—carts with two wheels pulled by men called coolies—and people being carried in painted sedan chairs.

Mei Fuh hitched herself up in Adjipah's arms to see the canal better and watch the sampans being poled along. The poles went *swish, swish* as men pushed and pulled the flat boats through the water. Under their little roofs were vegetables and fruit and brightly colored lanterns being carried to market to be sold. Sometimes there were other things too.

"Look! A pink pig riding to market! At least it's pink in between the dirt," said Mei Fuh.

Sometimes there were parades with enormous dragons and idols with frightening frowns. Even though the dragons were made of paper and the idols were carved from wood, Mei Fuh was glad to be safe in Adjipah's arms behind the gate. There were always firecrackers at the parades, and she loved to hear them go *bang, bang, swoosh!* There were little rockets, too, and they went *whish, whoosh, BANG!* in a spray of red sparks.

One day Amah took Mei Fuh for a walk outside the compound. Along the street beside the canal, she heard shouts and bangs and people making music on Chinese stringed instruments. The arguments and polite conversations were spoken in Chinese, which sounds a little like singing. People were cooking outside in front of their houses, and Mei Fuh smelled onions frying and fish cooking. She smelled pork balls sizzling in hot oil and banana fritters frying, mixed with the smell of firecrackers that had just gone *BANG!* and the smell of wood being carved and glued and painted. All the odors mixed together into one strange, wonderful, exciting fragrance.

Mei Fuh asked Amah questions.

"Amah, why is that wall there and another wall behind it? I want to see inside the door."

Amah explained, "That doorway leads to a room where carved idols sit, great big idols like the ones in the parades, except these are made of stone or brass. People believe that demons might go inside and spoil the idols. They also believe the

demons are very stupid and can't turn a corner. So they make crooked entrances, like a maze, with a wall that makes you turn left and a wall that makes you turn right, to keep out the stupid demons who can walk only in a straight line!"

Mei Fuh sniffed the air outside the doorway. She could smell the incense that always burned in front of the idols. *That incense can go around corners all right,* she thought.

Then she saw something else. "Look at that baby's funny hat! Why does it have such ugly monsters embroidered on it?"

"I'll tell you why," Amah said. "Baby boys are given the hats because their parents think the monster faces will scare demons away and keep the baby safe."

Mei Fuh walked along thinking about demons. She was comforted by Amah's reassuring hand holding hers, and by remembering something her parents had taught her from the Twenty-third Psalm: "The Lord is my shepherd." She was happy to see Adjipah waiting at the gate to their own compound. There was no need to be afraid.

The Goldfish

Mei Fuh had a pet goldfish that lived in a little pool of water in the garden. She loved to sit in the grass with the breeze in her face and watch the flash of orange-gold as the fish swam round and round, opening and shutting its mouth.

One day Mei Fuh and her mother and father left for a vacation at the seaside. As they left the compound Mei Fuh called, "Good-bye, Amah! Good-bye, Adjipah! Please take care of my goldfish till I come back. Oh . . . and thank you!"

The China Sea was nothing like the smooth pool where her goldfish lived. Mei Fuh was frightened by the big waves, even when her father held her in his arms. "Tomorrow I'll go in the water," she said, and she found a place in the sun where she could stand on one toe and twirl around. The salty air smelled good and she liked the taste of salt on her lips. As she twirled she thought of her goldfish, safe in the quiet water of the pool.

But back in the garden, Adjipah sat by the pond feeding the goldfish, sighing. He thought, *Oh, how good this goldfish would taste fried in a little oil with green onions and candied ginger. What a waste to sit here and feed it.*

Then Adjipah thought, *Maybe Mei Fuh will never come back . . . Maybe the world will come to an end . . . Maybe, just maybe I will die . . . And what a waste it would be not to enjoy the fish first . . .*

Adjipah jumped up and hurried away to find a net. He hurried back and swished it around in the pond for a while, first on one side, then on the other. *Flip-flop* . . . almost . . . and then the fish was in the net, still flopping.

Before he could change his mind, Adjipah found

a frying pan, some fresh scallions, a jar of candied ginger, some soy sauce, and the right oil, along with a sharp knife and a cutting board. He chopped the onions, sliced the ginger into paper-thin slices, and stirred up the fire in the big black stove. While the frying pan and oil were growing hot, he prepared the fish, determined not to think of Mei Fuh.

"Mmmm!" Adjipah said as picked up his chopsticks and took a bite. "This is good. It's going to be perfect. What a waste it would be to have such a delicious goldfish just swimming round and round in a pond!"

When Mei Fuh came back from the beach, she hurried through the compound, ran along a path, and knelt on the edge of the pond, looking into the water.

"Where are you?" she called to the fish. Then a bit louder and anxiously: "Where *are* you?" But there was no flash of red-gold. The water was too empty and too still.

Mei Fuh ran from one little house to another. "Has anyone seen my goldfish?" she asked everyone. She ran to all the houses in the compound, but no one answered.

Mei Fuh went out to the bamboo grove to hide her tears—and to twirl. Twirling was her favorite thing to do. Soon the little breeze took her frown away.

Mei Fuh could see only a small piece of sky through the bamboo trees. It seemed to belong to her . . . her own outdoor ceiling. She felt a little lonely and wished she were up there, floating free with the clouds. Her straight Chinese pants would not puff out like a cloud. Still, when she was very happy or very sad or missing her goldfish, twirling always made her feel much better.

Amah's Fan

Summer days in Wenchow were so hot and humid that Mei Fuh's clothes stuck to her back when she leaned back in a chair. Even in bed she felt sweaty. Everyone in China used fans. People brought their fans to church and to theaters. They fanned themselves in little boats as they went down the river and in rickshaws and sedan chairs as they went down the street.

Mei Fuh saw beautiful fans with delicately carved ivory spokes, silk fans with painted pictures, and folding fans with jewels and silver. But Amah's big bamboo leaf fan was Mei Fuh's favorite.

When it was hot and still at bedtime and no breeze moved the curtains, Amah settled herself in a rocking chair by Mei Fuh's bed with her big fan in her hand. This was a signal to Mei Fuh.

She said her prayers with her mother. Then she jumped into bed and lay quietly, trying not to wiggle. Thoughts were humming and popping inside her head. "When you stop moving around, I can begin," Amah said.

The chair squeaked as Amah rocked herself. *Rock, squeak. Rock, squeak. Rock, squeak.* Then she started to sing a song that sounded to Mei Fuh like "Neee-naah, neee-naah. Nnneeee. Nnnaaah."

Mei Fuh waited, not moving even one toe. At last Amah said, Mei Fuh is such a good girl, so quiet and ready for sleep. Now I can begin!

Amah kept rocking and singing, but now she added something more. This is what Mei Fuh had been waiting for. Amah picked up her wheat-colored fan and added a new beat. With five fast little whooshes of the fan, Amah fanned her own face, making five little breezes. Then—*SWOOSH!*

A great powerful wind blew over Mei Fuh. Amah stayed a long time, fanning Mei Fuh until she fell asleep.

This is how Mei Fuh learned to count: "One whoosh, two whoosh, three whoosh, four whoosh, five whoosh, six SWOOSH!"

Kites and Afternoon Tea

Mei Fuh liked to fly kites with her friend, a girl named Bang Tsau. Mei Fuh even liked to say "Bang Tsau" because the *ts* sound had to be made with her tongue behind her upper teeth and it felt nice. Mei Fuh and Bang Tsau had wonderful box kites that Adjipah and the cook had made for them from thin strips of wood and a special strong paper with pictures on it. The feathery light boxes had long, long tails so they would fly well.

Amah helped them get their kites up in the air.

Outside the wall, boys were flying their plain paper kites up, up, up. Suddenly the boys jerked their kite strings so their kites dipped down and the strings twisted around the girls' kite strings. Then, very quickly, the boys rolled up their strings, like fishermen pulling in fish, and the beautiful box kites disappeared over the wall.

Mei Fuh and Bang Tsau cried, but soon Mei Fuh jumped up and danced around to cheer herself up. Inside her, little bubbles like sparkling water bubbled up and she felt happy again. Outside, nothing whirled around her except a little breeze and the piece of kite string she still held tightly in her fingers. The garden was empty. The sky was empty of kites . . . but there was a small white cloud floating on its own.

Mei Fuh had another friend named Nina. She lived in a compound far across the city. Dressed in her favorite Chinese pants and top, Mei Fuh would wait with Amah inside the gate for the moment when it swung open and she and Amah climbed into a waiting rickshaw. Over the cobblestone streets and dirt roads, the big wheels bumped as the coolie ran.

Mei Fuh was afraid as she rode in the rickshaw because its wheels sometimes ran over a chicken or nearly hit a cat. The coolie wore a big straw hat and he always looked down at the street so he would not step on a nail or a piece of broken pottery. He never looked to see who was in front of him but just ran and ran. People walking with baskets of fish on their heads and children playing games scurried to get out of his way.

Mei Fuh liked to visit Nina, but she didn't like the rickshaw ride. "Please look out! Oh, be careful!" she called out as the coolie knocked over a little boy. The boy's big sister snatched him up and shook her fist at the man. He kept running as though nothing had happened.

When she got to Nina's house, their amahs prepared a picnic on two trays.

"Goody! Tea!" Nina cried.

"With zingdaw and buffalo cream for our toast!" said Mei Fuh.

"Tea" wasn't just tea to drink; it was the name of an afternoon meal. Zingdaw was a wonderful thick malt syrup to spread on the toast. Buffalo cream came from buffalo milk. It was so thick that it could be spread on top of the zingdaw like whipped cream. Zingdaw and buffalo cream were special treats.

The amahs spread a cloth on a low round table on the grass and put down a pot of cambric tea, a weak tea with lots of milk and sugar. There was a small cream pitcher, a dish with sugar, teacups and saucers of thin china, embroidered napkins, and fancy little silver spoons. It was a lovely proper tea.

Mei Fuh and Nina sat on the grass and pretended they were the two English ladies they had seen when they had afternoon tea with their parents in Shanghai.

"Will you have a little sugar?" asked Nina.

"Yes, thank you very much, and more toast and zingdaw, please."

They stuck their little fingers out when they held their teacups, thinking it looked more elegant. Mei Fuh taught Nina to offer tea and toast in English, since they were pretending to be English ladies. But soon they giggled and went back to chattering in Chinese, which was more natural for both of them.

A Terrible Accident
and Some Presents

Every morning Mei Fuh took a bath. Amah would put a tin bathtub in the middle of Mei Fuh's room with a thick towel on the floor beside it. She put another towel on a chair and Pears soap on a table with a washcloth and talcum powder. Then she got the water from the pump.

Usually Amah brought the cold water first and put the pail by Mei Fuh's door. Then she would get the hot water, which had been heating on the black coal-burning stove in the kitchen. Mei Fuh was

24

supposed to wait in bed until Amah had mixed
both pails of water in the tub. When Amah shut the
door, that was the signal for Mei Fuh to get up. But
one morning, Amah brought the boiling water first
and *that* was the morning Mei Fuh decided to pour
her own bath water. She slid out of bed, ran over to
the pail of water, and tried to lift it. Of course it was
too heavy and . . . *ooww!* The pail fell against Mei
Fuh, knocking her down, and boiling hot water

spilled over her legs.

"Mummy! Amah!" Mei Fuh screamed in pain. Amah came running to see what had happened and picked her up. Then her mother came, and Dr. Stediford, who put a thick layer of gooey yellow ointment all over her legs, covering the burns. He wrapped big soft bandages around her legs until they looked like they were in casts.

For many weeks Mei Fuh couldn't walk. Even when she didn't move, her legs hurt. She lay on a big chair so her legs could go straight out in front of her. Amah fanned her with the bamboo leaf fan and told her stories in Chinese. Her mother read her stories in English. And the people who lived in the compound brought her presents to cheer her up.

One present was a white rabbit—a real live one! Another present was a fuzzy baby goat. Mei Fuh couldn't play with that bouncy present until her legs got better. But the most surprising present was a large flat basket of tiny worms with another basket of fresh mulberry leaves and a pair of scissors.

"Worms and leaves!" said Mei Fuh. "What for?"

The worms were silkworms that spin silk thread.

The leaves were food for the worms. The very best silk comes from silkworms that have eaten only mulberry leaves, people told Mei Fuh.

"Cut the mulberry leaves into tiny slivers and spread them in the leaf basket," said Mei Fuh's mother. Amah helped. Then they picked up the wiggly worms and put them on the leaves. Many times each day Amah and Mei Fuh cut up leaves for the worms to eat. As the worms grew bigger, the pieces of leaf didn't have to be so small.

"Listen!" Mei Fuh said to everyone who came to visit her. Everyone listened. They heard a soft *rustle rustle, nibble nibble*—the sound of silkworms moving on the leaves and chewing. Amah would nod or the doctor would say, "I didn't know this was a laboratory." While Mei Fuh waited for her legs to get better, she fed the silkworms and listened to them. They were better than toys because they were real. They were real silkworms getting ready to make real silk.

The rabbit grew. The kid ran and jumped. The worms got bigger and bigger until they could eat whole leaves that hadn't been cut up at all. Then one day the doctor took the bandages off Mei Fuh's legs. She could run and jump and climb and whirl and twirl. Finally!

Mei Fuh climbed into an old rowboat in the garden under the bamboo trees and pulled the baby goat in with her. "Aaalll aboard for Shang-hai!" she called, rowing the grass with one oar.

Baby goats have horns growing underneath the skin on their heads, and they run around lowering their heads looking for something to butt. Mei Fuh and the kid liked to butt each other. They'd bump their heads together—little bumps that didn't hurt. Then one day they butted each other, *bump, bump, bump,* and "Ouch, ouch, OUCH!" cried Mei Fuh.

The kid's horns had come through, like a baby's teeth coming through its gums. For a while Mei Fuh had two sore bumps on her head, exactly as far apart as the kid's horns. After that, the kid went to live on a farm where it could bump heads with other goats.

All this time, Mei Fuh had been taking good care of her silkworms. She had fed them until they were so big that they had stopped eating. This meant it was time for them to start spinning cocoons.

Mei Fuh and Amah placed thin dry branches in the worms' basket with plenty of twigs for the worms to attach themselves to. Thin threads of silk were soon coming out of each worm and being spun round and round, until each worm was enclosed in a silk cocoon. The cocoons were creamy white balls attached all over the branches, but Mei

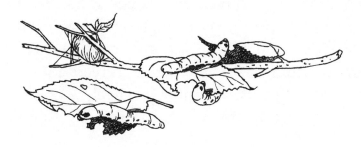

Fuh knew there was a worm inside each one. The cocoons were getting bigger and bigger without anyone's touching them. It was very mysterious.

"This is where silk comes from," Mei Fuh's mother told her. "Round and round it winds."

Mei Fuh and Amah had been able to feed the worms and give them branches, but they couldn't tell when the cocoons were ready to be unwound. A woman who had worked with silkworms for many years came to Mei Fuh's house. She took a cocoon, held it up to a light, and looked at it very carefully. It was transparent. She said it was just right.

The woman had brought a huge black kettle, which was put over a coal-burning stove. The fire was made and the water started to boil. Then a spinning wheel was set up beside her chair.

Mei Fuh watched in astonishment as the woman used chopsticks to pick up a cocoon that had been bobbing up and down in the boiling water. With a little twist (which you couldn't copy even if you were watching) she worked a thread loose and attached it to her spinning wheel. The thread unwound from the cocoon onto the spinning

wheel just as a spool of thread unwinds from a sewing box.

Mei Fuh's silk thread was taken away to be woven on a loom into silk fabric and dyed blue. Then came the next exciting day. A sewing woman came and spread the soft blue fabric on a table and cut it into shapes, just the right shapes to make a dress for Mei Fuh. What fun to watch and dream about! What kind of dress would it be?

At last the dress was finished and Amah buttoned up all the little buttons. When Mei Fuh felt the delicious touch of the silk on her skin, she ran outside. She spun around, but the dress was a narrow Chinese dress with slits on each side. It remained straight, as straight as her little cotton pants. Still, it was special—and soft as a cloud.

"How pretty!" said Amah

"How pretty!" said Adjipah.

"How pretty," said Mummy. "And just think, you grew that silk yourself!"

Eating Lessons

Mei Fuh liked to watch people working in the kitchen, but she had to be careful not to get in the way.

One day, Mei Fuh watched Wong make an American recipe for birthday cake icing. First Wong boiled water and sugar together in a pan. Then he took six chopsticks in his right hand and spread them out like a fan. After he separated the eggs, he put the whites on a platter and began whipping them with the chopsticks, moving his hand and the sticks so fast that they blurred. Soon the egg whites became thick and stood up in peaks. A boy who helped in the kitchen poured a stream of the hot sugar syrup on the egg whites as Wong beat them. Up, up went the egg whites, smoother and whiter, until they were ready to be spread on the cake.

"What a lot of things chopsticks can do," said Mei Fuh to Mei Yong as they licked the icing off the chopsticks. "They can take cocoons out of boiling water, get the silk going on the spinning wheel, and beat egg whites to make icing that looks like a fluffy cloud that you can eat."

When dinner was cooked, Wong scrubbed a block of wood clean. Sometimes the block held pans with puffed rice patted down in them. Meats and vegetables were chopped, shredded, and piled in neat heaps. They looked like a picture painted in beautiful colors. The shredded Chinese cabbage was pale yellow-green. Peppers, cut thin as shoelaces, were dark green. Thin, round slices of onion were white next to dark brown ruffles of Chinese mushrooms. The raw beef was a different shade of pink than the raw veal. The smells teased Mei Fuh's nose as she watched Wong cook over his glowing iron stove.

Mei Fuh and her mother had different ideas about food. Her mother thought that Chinese food was too rich for children. She told Amah to give Mei Fuh boring things like a soft-boiled egg with toast fingers and jam. Friday was the only day Mei Fuh could have a bowl of rice and some Chinese food to eat with chopsticks.

But Mei Fuh thought, *I love Chinese food. I love to eat with chopsticks. I'm going to visit my Chinese friends when they are eating and maybe . . .*

Mei Fuh began to appear on the doorsteps of

the houses in the compound just as the rice was being dished into bowls and steaming plates of vegetables and fish were placed on the table. As someone came to the door to greet her, she would bow politely and shake hands. But she didn't shake the other person's hand, she shook her own! It was not polite to touch another person's hands. Instead, Chinese people clasped their own hands in front of them and gave them a little shake. Mei Fuh knew how to do this, just as she knew how to shake hands with English and American people.

Then Mei Fuh would look up and smile, and someone would say, "Come, Mei Fuh, sit here." Kind hands lifted her up on a bench next to another child, put a bowl of rice in front of her, and gave her a pair of chopsticks. Steaming cabbage, water chestnuts, and green pea pods were given to her, and someone in the family put a piece of white fish on top of Mei Fuh's rice with his chopsticks. This was a polite way of welcoming a guest.

"Mmmmm," said Mei Fuh. "I'm sure this food is good for me. It feels good in my tummy." The family would nod their heads in approval.

One family after another began to watch for Mei

Fuh at mealtimes. Usually someone sat outside on the bench by the door to wait for her. They liked to teach her how to use chopsticks and how to take food out of the big bowls with the ends that had not been in her mouth.

One woman, Mrs. Liu, and her family thought Mei Fuh should also learn to drink tea while eating a mouthful of rice. This was a special skill that Mei Fuh would need all her life, they said. The whole family stood around Mei Fuh to give her instructions.

"Hold your bowl of rice near your face and scoop some into your mouth. Now hold your chopsticks together like this. Don't chew the rice; pat it with the chopsticks over to the left. Pat it firmly in your left cheek," Mrs. Liu said. "Now open your mouth and let us look."

Everyone crowded around. "Oh, look how well she's done it!"

"Now, take your tea and sip it on the right side of your mouth. See? You can sip tea without moving a single grain of rice. Then you can chew the rice without being thirsty."

Mei Fuh skipped home. She was so excited that

she sang, "I can sip tea without 'sturbing the rice. What do you say now? Isn't that nice?"

Mei Fuh learned something else as well. Every day Wong bought food from peddlers who came to the gate with baskets of vegetables and fruits on their heads. Wong would ask the price. Then he would offer less money. The peddler would shake his head in horror and name another price a little lower than his first one. This bargaining would go

on for quite a long time before the money was paid and Wong's basket was full.

Mei Fuh spoke Chinese so well that Wong, Amah, Mrs. Liu, and Adjipah taught her how to bargain with the peddlers. She learned to say, "Oh, I wouldn't pay that many cash for those onions. Oh, no, no, they are very inferior onions. I will pay only this many cash." Chinese cash consisted of coins with a hole in the middle, carried on a string. Mei Fuh pointed out how many, copying the way Wong would shake his head, looking scornfully at the onions or oranges. Back and forth, Mei Fuh bargained with the peddler until the price was agreed on.

The cook and Amah and Mrs. Liu and the others would laugh and clap their hands to see little Mei Fuh bargain so well.

As she ran back to her bamboo trees to twirl around, Mei Fuh sang an English song from her nursery rhyme book: "Oranges and lemons, say the bells of Saint Clemens."

"Fly, Little Bug"

Mei Fuh loved to sing and hum when she twirled. The tunes that she sang were a strange mixture of English and Chinese. Mei Fuh's mother taught her some rhymes to sing. She knew:

Baa, baa black sheep, have you any wool?
Yes, sir, yes, sir, three bags full.

and

*Mary had a little lamb, little lamb, little
  lamb,
Mary had a little lamb, its fleece was white as
  snow.*

I wonder, thought Mei Fuh, *if Mary's lamb ever
grew horns to bump her with.*

There was a pump organ in the living room of Mei Fuh's house. She was still too small to play it. To play the organ, one had to have legs long enough to pump the foot pedals while playing the keys. It was a little like trying to rub your stomach and pat your head at the same time. Mei Fuh tried *that* once, watching someone play the organ.

But most of the music she heard was Chinese music played on Chinese instruments, or songs and chants that Amah sang. Mei Fuh learned all sorts of Chinese songs. Her favorite was one that Amah taught her, which needed two people to sing and laugh over:

*Ti jong jong
Ti jong jong
Jong jong*

Fee kee
Fee kee fee nauw dau?
Fee kee
Mei Fuh
Bi-du-kong!

It means something like:

Fly little bug!
Fly little bug!
Little bug, fly away where?
Fly away to
Mei Fuh's
nose!

43

As you sing "Ti jong jong," you pinch the back of your own hand. As you sing "Jong jong Fee kee," you flutter your hands in air like a bug flying. At the end of the song, you touch the other person's nose and say the other person's name.

Mei Fuh sang "Amah's Bi-du-kong!" and touched Amah's nose. Mei Fuh and Amah laughed and laughed. Then they sang it again.

Pilgrim's Progress

Mei Fuh's big sisters, Mei Yong and Mei Oe, came home from boarding school for their long winter vacation. The coastal steamer brought them to Shanghai from North China; then a smaller boat carried them to Wenchow.

Mei Fuh was happy when they were home. Mei Oe was always busy reading her own books and writing letters, but Mei Yong loved to read to Mei Fuh. She would choose a book from the big shelf and they would settle into chairs in the nursery. Mei Yong's favorite was *Pilgrim's Progress*.

"Let's play Pilgrim," Mei Yong said one day when Amah was changing the sheets on the beds. Mei Yong pulled two pillowcases from the pile and handed one to Mei Fuh. "Here, push a sheet into your pillowcase, like this, and then bumpy things like shoes and blocks." Mei Yong explained that these stood for anything naughty she had done lately.

"I'm going to put my wooden box in mine and this twirly top," said Mei Fuh. She thought of her secret visits at mealtimes as she hoisted the heavy bag on her back.

"Hold a corner of the pillowcase like this, over your left shoulder, see?" Mei Yong showed her little sister. "We'll pretend the stairs are a hill full of stones and thorns. We must carry our burdens up the hill before we can let them go." The two girls started up the mahogany staircase, puffing and blowing. When they got to the top, Mei Yong whispered, "Now let go, Mei Fuh." Their bags went *bump bump* down the stairs and spilled out at the bottom. They played again and again.

Mei Fuh felt so light after "losing her burdens" that she ran out into the garden. She found a smooth place near her favorite bamboo tree. Round and round she whirled, balanced on one foot with her arms outstretched. Mei Yong laughed to see Mei Fuh concentrating so hard.

Hmm, thought Mei Fuh, not saying anything out loud. *It is nice to have a big sister to play with but I wish I could twirl in the sky with the clouds.*

Staying Warm

On Sundays, Mei Fuh and her family went to church in the compound. As they slid into their places on the benches, many other people crowded in also, from outside the compound as well as inside. But there was no heat in the big room, and it was cold, damp, and shivery.

They all wore padded clothes to keep warm because the houses weren't any warmer than the church. Their clothes were made like a quilt: two layers of cloth were sewn with a fat layer of cotton padding in between. Even their shoes were made with padded cloth. People kept their clothes on for the whole winter. The pants had a slit in the bottom so they could go to the toilet without taking anything off, but the jackets were so long that the slit did not show.

Mei Fuh and her sisters and parents wore padded clothes, but they could take them off at night, just like all their other clothes. They also had long woolen underwear sent from England by a friend.

Their thick clothing still could not keep people warm in church, however, so each person brought along his or her own heat. The heat came from tiny stoves for their feet and even tinier stoves for their hands. The stoves were brass or copper boxes. Their lids looked like beautiful metal lace, with holes punched in designs of flowers and leaves. They had handles so one wouldn't burn his or her hands carrying them. Inside were red-hot coals from kitchen stoves.

Mei Fuh's handwarmer and footwarmer kept her cozy all through the singing and preaching and praying. Soon the whole big room was warmed up

by all the tiny stoves. What nice, comforting heat!

After church, Mei Fuh took her handwarmer and walked to the verandah with Mei Yong. "Let's play a game until dinner," Mei Yong suggested.

"What game?" asked Mei Fuh.

"Let's play bound feet," said Mei Yong. "You saw those women after church, standing and talking to each other. Did you see how the ones with bound feet can't stand still? They have to keep taking little steps, like this." And Mei Yong took off her shoes and stood on her heels with her ankles bent and her toes turned up. Mei Fuh tried it too. *Teeter, teeter, wobble* went the girls, around in little circles, trying to stand still but finding it almost impossible. This wasn't a bit like the freedom of running and skipping.

"Oh dear, those women couldn't ever whirl and twirl, could they? They can't stop the game and do something else. Their feet just stay that way, and it hurts. What happened to their feet, Mei Yong?"

"Chinese people believe that women are prettier if they have very tiny feet," said Mei Yong. "When girls are young, their toes are bent underneath and wrapped up tight in bandages so they won't grow. Only farm girls or servants have unbound feet, so they can work."

Mei Fuh and Mei Yong sat down and looked at their toes and wiggled them. Then they sighed. Jumping up, they walked on their heels in tiny wobbly steps, then flung out their arms and stood on their toes. Mei Fuh shouted, "Oh, I'm glad I have free toes that can whirl and kick and run. Toes are really important!"

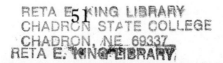

Then they walked to dinner across the verandah, holding each other's hands, thinking their own thoughts.

The City Wall

Mei Fuh went for long walks with Mei Yong and Amah. They would go out to the city wall, which was very high and so thick that there were houses on top and a path to walk on.

Walking to the wall, Mei Fuh watched people work. Almost everything was made by hand in people's houses, even when the houses had only one room. Workshops spilled out onto the sidewalk or the street because there wasn't enough space inside. A sewing machine might be in a doorway, and a table to cut out jackets, pants, and dresses would be against the wall of the building.

In the streets there might be a woman with her arms stretched out, being measured for a jacket, and someone else being measured for a pair of pants.

Outside their homes people had little pots of paint for painting drums or wedding sedan chairs. They held different sizes of paintbrushes in their mouths so that people walking by wouldn't bump into them.

People made chopsticks, coffins, lanterns, clothing, and shoes right in the open where everyone could see. No one in China would think that shoes grew in boxes in the shoe store or that eggs were made in a factory. Everybody knew where things came from, and they knew who made them or grew them.

Mei Fuh had a favorite workshop—the one where umbrellas were made. "Oh, smell the umbrellas. I love that smell!" Mei Yong and Amah took deep breaths, smelling the scent of the oil used to waterproof the brown paper of the umbrellas. Umbrellas kept that special smell for as long as they could be used.

Mei Fuh, Mei Yong, and Amah smelled the oil as they stood and watched umbrellas being made. A man cut long, very thin wooden sticks, and another man cut shorter, fatter sticks. A woman painted the thin sticks green and a boy added red tips to the green sticks. Sections of brown paper were oiled and then put aside to dry until they were the color of old oak leaves. The dry pieces were stitched together. Then thirty-seven long spokes were glued to each circle of oiled paper. "It really is an umbrella now!" cried Mei Fuh. "What a beautiful round shape."

When the umbrella was closed, it was green because of the green spokes and fat because of the paper. It made a good cane to lean on or to swing by the string through the hole in its handle.

Mei Fuh loved the round, graceful circle that stretched straight out and she loved the handle of bamboo, but most of all she loved the fragrance. The umbrella smelled even better, she thought, when it was wet, the rain pattering down on the tightly stretched paper to make that certain cozy sound. It was like having a private roof that could be carried everywhere.

"Look up there!" said Mei Yong. "See all those bamboo poles?"

Mei Fuh and Amah looked. Poles stuck out of windows and across the street. Each pole displayed a row of drying clothes, but the clothes weren't hung with clothespins. Instead, the pole came through the sleeves of each shirt and through one leg of each pair of pants. "They look like paper dolls in a row," said Mei Fuh.

The street was full of wheelbarrows, rickshaws, and people. Babies crawled, children ran, and men hammered things. Mei Fuh twirled around a bit— just in her head. She might kick something over if she wasn't careful!

As Amah, Mei Fuh, and Mei Yong came nearer the city wall, Mei Fuh heard quiet crying sounds inside a pagoda with latticework walls.

"Amah, what is that?"

Amah answered, "Oh, those are baby girls, newborn baby girls that have been thrown away. Their mamas wanted boys. They didn't want girls." Amah spoke very calmly.

"But Amah," Mei Fuh said. "I'm a girl, and my mummy and daddy already had two girls when I was born. And their boy baby, my brother, had died. My mummy and daddy wanted a boy, and they got me."

Mei Fuh was angry and scared, but she also felt like crying. *I wish somebody had loved those little girls,* she thought. *I'm a girl. I like to whirl around. I like to sing. I like to smell Chinese umbrellas and eat zingdaw with cream. Those are girls just like me.* Then she started to cry.

Amah patted Mei Fuh. "Your mama and daddy love God and they love you. They wouldn't throw away a little person. They believe that's wrong."

Mei Fuh walked on and on, thinking. Soon there was something unusual to look at, something that didn't go down the street every day: a Chinese wedding.

Mei Fuh, Mei Yong, and Amah moved out of the way as men with poles on their shoulders carried the wedding sedan chair by. The chair was bright red lacquer and decorated all over with pieces of mirrors, colored glass jewels, and bits that looked like gold and silver. There were heavy cloth curtains trimmed with gold fringe and embroidery that hid the bride.

"I wish I could see the bride," said Mei Fuh. "I wonder what she looks like."

"I saw a bride once," said Mei Yong. "She was one of the schoolgirls from the compound."

Amah had seen many brides. "A bride has a very high headdress, sort of like a tall crown. It looks heavy and is covered with pieces of mirror and shiny stones and fringes, all red and blue and green and gold and silver. A bride wears a dress like a red tunic over red pants. It has embroidery all over it and a wide belt decorated with little mirrors and glass pieces. Everything sparkles."

Mei Yong said, "Even the bride's shoes are covered with sparkles, but you can't see them, because they're under her tunic. Oh, and the wedding feast! There are so many good things to eat, out of special bowls. You ought to taste the pork balls."

Mei Fuh went to bed that night with a jumble in her mind of brides in red clothes with mirrors on their belts, umbrellas smelling like their special oil, sedan chairs dazzling her eyes with decorations, and babies crying behind a thin wall.

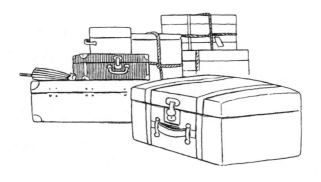

Boxes, Barrels, and Trunks

Mei Fuh thought that America must be a huge compound with lots of houses and beautiful gardens and a very high wall. That was all she had ever known. She knew she had just one grandfather; she knew her grandmothers had died as well as her other grandfather. But she imagined that this compound, America, was filled with houses of her relatives—aunts, uncles, cousins—as well as many smiling, friendly people who would be good neighbors. They would all be people who would understand that they should never throw away their baby girls.

So Mei Fuh was very happy and excited when her parents told her that the family was moving back to America because she would be seeing all sorts of relatives for the first time. She spun around in her room and by the bamboo trees, jumping in and out of her old rowboat. She ran up on the big porch and twirled on the smooth floor, humming her music.

As the days went by, the house looked different. Boxes, barrels, and straw suitcases were being packed. There were trunks with brass corners and leather bands attached with brass-headed nails. Carefully labeled packages were piled everywhere, waiting for someone to find the right place to put them.

Often Mei Fuh's father was the person who decided where to put things. He was called the champion packer, because he was so good at it. He folded clothes very neatly and rolled up soft towels to fit in any little spaces so that the whole box or suitcase would be tightly packed. "Then breakable things won't rattle around and get broken," he told

Mei Fuh. "You can't imagine how often a trunk gets thrown around, traveling in a boat."

Of course, they were traveling by boat. First they would ride a steamer up the coast to the city of Shanghai and then a bigger boat would take them on the long trip to America.

Mei Fuh watched the packing. "Don't forget my umbrella," she sang out. "It might rain in America. And my drum. Please pack my drum very carefully, Daddy." Her drum was blue with flowers on the sides and funny faces on the ends and a red silk cord so she could wear it around her neck.

Soon the books came out of the bookcase, and Mei Fuh sat on the floor to look at them and smell them. The hot damp weather gave the books a slight musty smell. Mei Fuh patted the books. "Good old smell. I'm glad we can take you to America with us." Then she went to watch her dolls being packed.

Finally it was time to leave.

It's hard to say good-bye, thought Mei Fuh. She had seen people cry when someone was going away for a long time. And sure enough, when everyone came to say good-bye, they felt like crying.

"Is Mei Fuh healthy?" asked Mrs. Liu.

"Oh, yes. Very healthy," answered Mei Fuh's mother.

"Well, she has eaten Chinese food every day for a long time," said Mrs. Liu. "And you can see it has been good for her."

So they told Mei Fuh's mother and father about her habit of appearing at mealtime, just as the rice was put on the table, and everyone laughed instead of crying. Then they told about teaching Mei Fuh to drink tea with the rice packed on one side of her mouth. They were proud that Mei Fuh would go far away to America knowing how to eat rice properly.

Mei Fuh was saying good-bye to the place she had lived for her whole life—almost six years. She didn't know what would happen next. She didn't know how wide the ocean was or how long the trip would be. It was difficult to say good-bye to Amah and the others. Her mind was swirling. Still, it was good that people laughed at the end.

Exploring

After Mei Fuh and her parents left Wenchow, they took a small boat up the coast to Shanghai. At the same time, Mei Fuh's sisters were coming down the coast on another steamer to meet them there. In Shanghai, the whole family would board the big boat that would take them to the United States.

Mei Fuh was glad to see her sisters. Mei Yong was almost ten and Mei Oe was almost fourteen as they stood on the busy dock watching everyone's trunks and suitcases and boxes hoisted up on the

ship. People spoke different kinds of Chinese, British English, American English, Swedish, French, German, Italian, and other languages. All around were the sounds of people whispering and shouting and running around. Strange new smells mixed with the salty tang of the ocean.

The boat looked huge. Mei Fuh and her sisters tilted back their heads so they could look up: up the wide sides, up past the railings, up to the smokestacks that spewed black smoke. The coal that made the smoke would make the boat take them from Shanghai to Japan (for more coal), across the ocean to Hawaii, and finally to San Francisco. The bow, the front of the boat, had big letters painted on it. They said *The China.* "That's the name of our boat," said Mei Fuh's father. "It has crossed the ocean many times."

As they stood on the deck and the boat moved slowly out of the Shanghai harbor, the boat's whistle blew. The sound was louder and deeper than anything Mei Fuh had ever heard. It was so loud that she could feel the sound right through her chest, as though the whistle were inside her, sad and beautiful.

Every day on *The China* was the same, yet every day was different. Mei Fuh and her family each had a deck chair with their name on it, and they each had brought a steamer rug to keep them warm on deck. Every morning after breakfast Mei Fuh sat in her deck chair, and someone tucked her in. Everyone else sat in their chairs, too. Then a waiter in a white jacket brought each passenger beef tea in a white china cup. Then another waiter brought salted crackers. In the afternoon, at four o'clock, everyone got back on their deck chairs and the waiters brought tea and cookies.

Mei Fuh loved beef tea and salted crackers and tea and cookies, but she grew tired of sitting. Her family always seemed to be reading books, even her sisters, so she began to explore the boat. First she explored by herself, but soon she met a boy who was also five. His name was Bobby.

Mei Fuh and Bobby walked along the decks trying not to bump into people's chairs. They ran along the halls outside the cabin doors and up and down the stairs between decks. The main staircase was wide with a smooth wooden banister. Sometimes they slid down the banister or bumped down the stairs on their bottoms, having a race. And all the time, they went on "explores," finding their way all over the ship.

One day they pushed against the cabin doors in the hallway. It was just for fun, because people locked their cabin doors. But as they pushed on one door, it swung open! Inside, the cabin was lovely. Everything was very neat, and there was a fancy bedspread and mirrors on the walls. On the table was a tall, round, shiny box; on it were pictures of blue, pink, yellow, green, and white candy sticks. The picture also showed a blue candy stick broken in half and full of chocolate. Mei Fuh had eaten chocolate, so she knew how good it was.

Mei Fuh and Bobby looked at each other and then walked slowly over to the table. Bobby opened the lid of the box. Up it came without sticking even a little.

"Ohhh . . ." whispered Mei Fuh.

"Ooooo . . ." whispered Bobby.

"They are so thin," said Mei Fuh.

"They are so shiny," said Bobby.

"They look like satin," said Mei Fuh.

"I wonder," whispered Bobby, "I wonder what they taste like."

Then they each reached out and took a stick of candy. They ate them very slowly, making them last a long time.

"Another one wouldn't be too much. Let's take a blue one this time."

"Now a yellow one, and let's bite into it this time."

"We'll just try one of each color."

Then, "The box still looks full," they agreed, putting the lid back on it. Softly they tiptoed out, pulling the door behind them.

Mei Fuh ran to an empty spot in the salon, the passengers' living room, to celebrate the delicious chocolates, but the bubbly feeling wouldn't come. She felt dry inside. Then she stopped. She began to walk slowly, heading toward her mother as if something was pulling her along. She told her mother what she had done.

"That was a very wrong thing to do," said Mei Fuh's mother. "You should never go into someone's cabin unless you've been invited and have asked me if it's all right. And you should never take anything that belongs to someone else. Now you must find that lady and say you're sorry."

Bobby was waiting for Mei Fuh. They walked very slowly to the cabin and tapped on the door. *Maybe she isn't here,* thought Mei Fuh. Then the door opened.

Mei Fuh took a deep breath and said very fast, to get it over with, "We came into your cabin and took some sweets out of that box and ate them. I'm sorry."

"I'm sorry, too," said Bobby.

The lady smiled down at them. Then she laughed and patted their heads. "Oh, I'm sorry, too," she said. "I'm sorry I was so selfish and didn't offer to share with you. Here, have some more. They are nice, aren't they?"

What a surprise! Mei Fuh and Bobby ran back to Mei Fuh's mother. "Mummy, guess what! It was all her fault for being selfish. She said so."

Mei Fuh ran to a quiet place and twirled. The happy bubbles came back. *I hope when I'm a grownup I'll be nice to children like that lady,* she thought.

A Typhoon

The first stop the boat made was in Nagasaki, in Japan. More people got on the boat there. Mei Fuh, Bobby, Mei Yong, Mei Oe, and all the adults stood by the railing to watch the coal being loaded. Slanting gangplanks stretched from the dock to the opening where people dumped the coal in a huge bin. The people coming up the planks carrying coal in cloth bags on their backs and shoulders and heads were all women. One at a time, they dumped the coal out of their bags and came down the gangplank, almost running, to get their next load.

At last all the coal was on the ship, and the whistle again blew its deep, sad, exciting note, and the ship sailed out into the ocean.

One day, after they had been traveling for about three weeks, the captain told the passengers, "We are skirting a typhoon." Mei Fuh didn't know what a typhoon was, but she soon found out.

High waves washed over the decks. The wind blew and blew and slashed rain against the portholes. The boat pitched and rolled. Pitching is when the boat goes up and down from bow to

stern like a rocking horse. Rolling is when the boat tips from side to side. Suddenly the portholes on one side of the boat are underwater, and then the boat rolls up, and for a minute one thinks, *Now it will be straight,* and then it keeps rolling down on the other side.

Everything on a ship changes during a typhoon.

People couldn't lie in their deck chairs or go for walks on deck. Ropes were fastened to brass rings in the walls so people could hold on to something when they had to walk from place to place. Fewer people went to meals, for they were seasick. And all the tabletops in the dining room had little fences around them to keep the dishes from sliding off and breaking.

Mei Fuh turned out to be a good sailor, which means she didn't get seasick. She kept right on enjoying her meals and beef tea and crackers, and she thought the ropes were fun to slide along. When the boat knocked her off her feet, she slid down the slanting floor as if she were sledding down a hill.

Most of the passengers and crew were glad when the typhoon was over. The sun came out, the sky was blue, the sea was calm, and the water became a beautiful dark turquoise green. Soon there was something new to be excited about: land was in sight!

Is This America?

The China had reached Hawaii. "No, this is not the United States," Mei Fuh's sisters told her. The year was 1920.

When Mei Fuh looked over the side of the boat, something strange was happening. People on the boat were throwing coins into the water and divers went underwater to catch them in their mouths. To get on a little boat to take them to shore, Mei Fuh had to climb down the side of *The China* on a long rope ladder. "Always keep a hand for yourself," a man told her. That meant that she should never let go with both hands at the same time, even for a second. This was fun, thought Mei Fuh, as she felt the ocean spray on her face and tasted salt on her tongue.

On shore, Mei Fuh had her first ride in a car, a taxi. It seemed like magic that the car could move all by itself with no coolies to pull it, like a rickshaw, and no men to carry it on poles, like a sedan chair.

At the top of a hill, Mei Fuh and her family looked down over the turquoise water with frothy white waves and down on palm trees, grass, and white houses with pink tile roofs. It looked beautiful and new. "Someday I'm going to live in that house," thought Mei Fuh, picking the house with the brightest flowers in its garden.

Then the taxi brought them back to the harbor, the little boat brought them back to the *The China*, and that night Mei Fuh slept snugly in her berth in her mother and father's cabin.

The China steamed into San Francisco Harbor at sunset one day, almost a month after it had left Shanghai. The orange-red and apricot sky seemed to welcome it.

Now, *this* is America, Mei Fuh's sisters said as two sturdy tugboats pushed *The China* into the dock. People on the dock waved. People on the boat rushed around with ropes and suitcases. The boat had been a whole private world. Now it felt more like a busy warehouse, delivering people and trunks and boxes. There were honking horns, creaking cranes, the deep blast of the boat whistle, the bangs of dropped boxes, the shouts of sailors and dock workers. Everything was strange and loud.

This is America, Mei Fuh said to herself, *but where is the compound? Where are our relatives?*

Finally they were on land, which seemed to pitch and roll. How wobbly Mei Fuh felt!

San Francisco was even more surprising than Hawaii had been. The streets looked strange and the buildings were the tallest she had ever seen. Everything looked gray.

In their hotel, a strange box took Mei Fuh and her family up to their rooms. Mei Fuh had never ridden an elevator before, with its metal doors that opened and shut like the jaws of an alligator. After

Mei Fuh had ridden up and down twice without getting off, the elevator man scolded her. "You can't just ride up and down," he said. "You have to be going somewhere to do something."

So Mei Fuh went up to the top floor and whirled around and around in the hall. Then she found a staircase and walked down to the next floor and whirled there.

"Now I've gone somewhere and done something," she thought. "I can go on the alligator again!"

Mei Fuh and her family had to take a train from San Francisco to Chicago and then change to the train that would take them to Cleveland. The train engines burned coal. Black smoke poured out of the smokestack. Black soot poured into the open windows and sifted under windows (even when they were closed) and got all over everything. But the train made wonderful sounds. The engines went *CHOO choo, CHOO choo, CHOO choo!* As the train went faster its wheels went *clack-clack, clack-clack, clackity-clack, clackity-clack.* The whistle added its own sound: *whoo-whoooo, whoo-whoooo!*

I love this train, thought Mei Fuh. *I could just live on this train forever.* She could feel the train's whistle inside her, seeming to trail out like smoke over the countryside behind them.

Every night the porter pulled their seats forward so that the backs fell down and made a bed. Each bed had heavy curtains for privacy. A kind of shelf pulled out from the wall near the ceiling and made a top bunk bed. That had curtains too. All this was done while people were in the dining car having dinner.

Mei Fuh slept by the window, and when the train slowed down she pushed the window shade up so that she could press her nose against the glass. When the train stopped at a station, she watched all the different people walk around or get

on or off the train. She wondered who they were. And she wondered if any of them came from China and knew her Amah.

Every morning the coal smoke and dust and cinders had to be brushed off their clothes. Sometimes people's faces got smudges on them. But worst of all was the time when Mei Fuh got a cinder in her eye. It hurt, and it had to be washed out with boric water in a little cup. Her mother gave her a clean hankie to pat her eye with, and a kind passenger gave her a whole pack of gum. "Thank you," she said, not quite sure what it was.

Her mother explained. "Take one stick and unwrap it. That's right. Now you can chew it, but don't swallow it. You just chew it and then spit it out." Then she went on reading her book.

A few minutes later, Mei Fuh said, "I'm all through with my gum."

"All five sticks?" asked her mother, very surprised.

"Oh, yes," Mei Fuh answered happily. "I chewed one and then spit it out. Then I chewed the next and spit it out. Then the next and the next. It didn't take long. It was very nice."

Journey's End

"Cleveland, Ohio! Cleveland, Ohio!" the conductor called out as he walked through the train.

Bags and suitcases were lifted down. Hands reached up to lift Mei Fuh down the steep steps. Suddenly she was surrounded by cousins. Soon now, she supposed, they would be going to the family compound.

Off they went in a big car, along city streets, up avenues with trees, until they stopped and turned up the driveway leading to a house. It was a lovely

85

house, with wonderful beds and soft pillows, delicious food, and a garden full of flowers. There were older cousins who asked Mei Fuh to speak Chinese. There were games to play on the living room rug beside a fireplace. It was all very interesting.

But there was no compound and no big wall. And there was no house that belonged to her family. This was not their home.

Mei Fuh went out into the back yard alone. She pretended that each bush was a house, like the little Chinese houses she had visited in her own compound. She pretended that the hollyhocks were rice bowls, and she laughed and talked in Chinese with friends in her pretend compound.

After a while, Mei Fuh heard music coming out of a window, and she went back into the house. She found a record player with a big horn and a crank to make the record spin around. Then the music came and there were voices, a man and a woman, singing mysterious words: "Carry me back to old Virginie."

Mei Fuh didn't know where "old Virginie" was, or why the people wanted to be carried "back to where the cotton grows," but the music was sad. She longed to go back too, back to the place she

loved. She cried for a few minutes, but then she began to sing softly to herself, and she went back out to the garden, still singing.

She found a place hidden by bushes with a patch of clipped green lawn. She began to twirl. She looked up at the sky. "I think that's the same cloud I saw in China. My feet came with me too! I can twirl in China or in America. I can imagine things and listen to music. I'm the same *me*, wherever I am."

Full Circle

Mei Fuh did miss the compound. She missed Amah and Adjipah and Mrs. Liu. She missed speaking Chinese and eating Chinese food. And she missed her name—Mei Fuh. Now that she was in America and going to American schools, everyone called her Edith, her American name.

Years passed. Mei Fuh rode on more trains. She visited more aunts and uncles and cousins and one grandfather. She and her family found a new home and Mei Fuh made new friends. She had her first delicious ice cream cone.

In school, Mei Fuh was chosen to dance in a performance. The students practiced and learned the steps, and on the appointed night they arrived in their costumes: velvet knee breeches and old-fashioned dresses with full skirts.

The beautiful music started, the "Minuet in G" by Beethoven. And so, at last, dancing with her American classmates, Mei Fuh felt her happiness float up from within and her soft skirt billow out around her as she danced, free as a cloud.